PRAISE FOR
— The Quest —

Darren Key is not only my good friend and frequent golf partner, he is a trusted voice for me when it comes to strategic stewardship practices. ***The Quest*** *is a terrific introduction to some subjects that are important, but often overlooked or outright ignored. Darren is a proven and reliable guide on the journey to financial health and freedom.*

—Pastor John Hampton, Journey Christian Church, Apopka, FL

This book is full of ancient wisdom and practical application. It is simple (though not necessarily easy), biblical, and practical. If you want financial freedom, read ***The Quest****.*

—Carl Kuhl, Lead Pastor of Mosaic Christian Church

Darren tackles some of the most critical issues our culture faces in the realm of finances. His practical and biblical approach to tithing, investing, and debt avoidance will change lives if applied. ***The Quest*** *is a great read, perfect for groups or individuals.*

—Joe Putting, Lead Pastor of Tomoka Christian Church

I didn't read ***The Quest****, —I devoured it. Darren Key provides a book that is a quick read and an incredible resource for Pastors and other Christian leaders who want their church to learn and live by these practical, Biblical stewardship principles. I thought I knew a lot about giving and investing, but each chapter revealed that there is much more that I can learn. Read it, live it and share it.*

—Dave Stone, former Pastor, Southeast Christian Church, KY

The QUEST

Your Journey to Financial Health that Honors God

by

DARREN R. KEY

with MARK ATTEBERRY

ACORN PUBLISHING

FROM THE TINY ACORN . . .
GROWS THE MIGHTY OAK

The Quest

Printed in the United States of America.

For information, address Acorn Publishing, LLC, 3943 Irvine Blvd. Ste. 218, Irvine, CA 92602
www.acornpublishingllc.com

Cover design by Damonza

Author photos by Rachel Key and Skip Stowers.

Interior design and digital formatting by Debra Cranfield Kennedy

Unless otherwise noted, Bible passages are from the New Living Translation.

ISBN—978-1-952112-67-6 (hardcover)
ISBN—978-1-952112-68-3 (paperback)
Library of Congress Control Number: 2021910530

DEDICATION

To my wife, Rachel:
Your love and commitment to our family
inspires me to be a better man,
leader, and servant of God.

INTRODUCTION

A Quest Worth Making

He who completes a quest does not merely find something. He becomes something.

—Lev Grossman

A quest, by definition, is a long or arduous search for something considered to be important or valuable. Since the days of Abraham, who packed up all his belongings and set out on a journey to an unknown land, people have gone on quests. In fact, the idea of an epic search pulls so hard on the human heart and imagination that history, literature, and pop culture have become filled with quest stories.

As a child, I'm sure you sat spellbound as Dorothy, Toto, and their three friends searched the Land of Oz for a mysterious Wizard. In elementary school, you learned about the California Gold Rush and our nation's quest to put a man on the moon. More recently, you likely became immersed in Harry Potter's quest to destroy the evil villain, Voldemort. At some point, you surely got caught up in Indiana Jones's quest to find the lost Ark of the Covenant or Frodo Baggins's quest to destroy the Ring of Power.

Nothing captures our collective imagination quite like the idea of a quest. And it's not hard to understand why. When someone goes on a quest, four things invariably happen.

First, he goes places he's never been. Often these places are wondrous and mysterious and, of course, dangerous.

Second, he encounters challenges he's never faced. Mountains, storms, monsters and villains abound, all of which test the quester's mettle like never before.

Third, he discovers abilities he's never used. He finds reserves of strength, courage, and cunning that were never needed in his humdrum, pre-quest existence.

And fourth, he finds something he never expected. This is the best part, the reason we want to tag along on these epic journeys. We sense that there's something out there just beyond the horizon that is bigger, better, and more life-changing than anything the quester has imagined.

Think about Dorothy, surrounded by Munchkins, standing on the platform, ready to board the hot air balloon that will take her from the Emerald City back to Kansas. In the beginning, her Holy Grail—the thing she was searching for—was simply a way to get home. She found it, yes, but she found so much more along the way: friendship, inspiration, and a completely different way of thinking about life, home, and family.

I'm challenging you to go on a quest of your own, a journey to find something most people don't have but wish they did. A search to find something that will dramatically change your life for the better. I'm talking about the quest to achieve complete financial health that not only provides for your future, but also honors God.

According to a November, 2019 article in Forbes, only 29% of Americans consider themselves financially healthy.[1] This means that seven out of ten Americans have more money going out than coming in, too much debt, too few investments, a lack of savings, and a heavy load of stress. Many are tip-toeing along the very edge of financial ruin, living one misfortune away from being wiped out, with no idea what to do about it.

If you're already financially healthy in a way that honors God, praise the Lord! You will still find wisdom or inspiration in this book that will help you become even better at handling your money. But if you *are* in that group of seven out of ten people who are not financially healthy, pay attention because I have bad news and good news.

The bad news is that I can offer you no easy fixes. We *love* easy fixes. It's why diet pills that promise to give you the body of an Olympic athlete without diet or exercise actually sell. But when it comes to achieving financial health that honors God, there's no magic pill, potion, platitude, or podcast.

The good news, however, is that financial health that honors God *does* exist. It's not some mythical entity like Bigfoot or the Loch Ness Monster. It *is* out there, and it *is* attainable. And I mean for everybody. Maybe you've always believed that the only hope you had of living free from financial stress was winning the Publishers Clearing House sweepstakes or Powerball. Not true! Anyone can find financial health that honors God.

But you're not going to find it where you're sitting now.

Where you're sitting right now is the problem. Maybe you had a tragic event or made some poor choices. It may have been unintentional, because you received bad counsel, or because no one ever taught you how to manage money, but that doesn't change the reality. And yes, you have a lot of company, which might make you feel a tiny bit better. But if you're financially unhealthy, you can be sure that nothing you've been doing holds any hope for a better future.

To find financial health that honors God, you're going to have to climb out of that hole and set out on a quest. Yes, it will take you to places you've never been. Yes, it will bring you face to face with challenges you've never experienced. Yes, it will force you to dig deep and discover abilities you didn't know you had. But in the end, it will put you right where you want to be. And yes, it will turn out better than you imagined, for what you will find at the end of your journey is not just financial health that honors God, but a brand new you. You'll be surprised at how you changed emotionally and spiritually along the way. You'll be surprised at how much healthier your lifestyle is. And you'll be surprised at how good it feels to finally have one of the most important areas of your life fixed. Without question, this is a quest worth making.

Let me explain why this is so important to me.

For over twenty years I have led Christian Financial Resources. CFR manages hundreds of millions of dollars for thousands of Christian families, businesses, and ministries. You can't do work like this without getting an up-close look at the challenges and struggles people face with their money. I'm talking about good, godly people who have the purest of intentions, but who, for whatever reason, struggle with financial matters. The calling I feel is to help such people. It's not a calling that came in a vision or an unusual cloud formation or a miraculous arrangement of letters in my alphabet soup. It came from the Bible:

> Command those who are rich in this present world not to be arrogant nor to put their hope in wealth, which is so uncertain, but to put their hope in God, who richly provides us with everything for our enjoyment. Command them to do good, to be rich in good deeds, and to be generous and willing to share. In this way they will lay up treasure for themselves as a firm foundation for the coming age, so that they may take hold of the life that is truly life.[2]

With this as my calling, I have been on a quest of my own to reach as many people as possible with the good news that financial health that honors God is attainable. I've been blessed to speak to tens of thousands of people every year about how to best use the financial resources God has entrusted to them for the time they are on this planet. This book is a part of that continuing mission, another way to reach people with information that will dramatically improve their lives and bring them more into line with God's will.

How about you?

Are you financially healthy? Maybe you're not on your deathbed, but are you walking with a limp, financially speaking? Do you have a hacking cough when it comes to money matters? Does your credit card balance give you a headache? If so, the rest of this book is dedicated to helping you get financially healthy, and doing it in a way that honors God.

I'm packed and ready to lead you on this quest. If you truly want a better life for yourself, get your stuff and let's go.

CHAPTER 1

Not in Kansas Anymore?

Which is the way back to Kansas?
I can't go the way I came.

—Dorothy, to Glinda, the Good Witch of the South

When Dorothy's storm-tossed house landed with a thud in Munchkin Land, she stepped out, looked around in wonder, and concluded that she wasn't in Kansas anymore. From that moment, she had one goal in mind: to find her way home.

If I asked you to name Dorothy's most important asset in her quest to get home to Kansas, what would you say? Do you think it was her natural grit and determination? (She certainly was one tough and courageous young lady.) Would you choose the brainless scarecrow, the heartless tin man, or the cowardly lion? (Those guys sure came through for her when everything was on the line.) Or maybe you'd say it was those beautiful ruby red slippers that she clicked three times to send her on her way?

As important as all of those things were, I'm voting for none of the above. I believe that, without question, Dorothy's biggest asset was that yellow brick road.

An old Chinese proverb says that a journey of a thousand miles begins with a single step. Have you ever wondered how many thousand-mile journeys have turned into fifteen hundred or two thousand miles or even more because the first step was taken in the wrong direction? If Dorothy hadn't had the yellow brick road to follow, would she *ever* have found her three friends or the Emerald City or the mysterious Wizard of Oz? Perhaps, but it would likely have taken her a lot longer and she surely would have suffered a great deal more.

If you're one of the seven out of ten people I mentioned in the introduction who are not financially healthy, you can probably relate very well to Dorothy's predicament. You probably feel lost and confused, just like she did. You may be wondering how you ended up where you are and how in the world you're ever going to get home to your happy place, financially speaking. One thing is certain: the last thing you want to do is start out in the wrong direction. You want for yourself a first-class, Grade-A, can't-miss yellow brick road to follow. The good news I have to share with you in this chapter is that you have one. It's more commonly known as the Bible.

Psalm 37:23 says, "The LORD directs the steps of the godly." How does he do this? Some might say with visions or dreams or miraculous signs and wonders. But if that were true, why would so many godly people struggle with their finances? Who would ever make a foolish impulse buy if lightning flashed and a voice boomed out of the heavens saying, "Put that credit card away!" No, the way God directs the steps of the godly is through his Word.

Second Timothy 3:16 says, "All Scripture is inspired by God and is useful to teach us what is true and to make us realize what is wrong in our lives. It corrects us when we are wrong and teaches us to do what is right." Do you see it? God's Word is the thing we can depend on to keep us from veering off track and getting lost on our journey. It is our yellow brick road.

This is why the organization I lead has the word "Christian" in its name. We could be Trustworthy Financial Resources or Dependable Financial Resources or Abundant Financial Resources, but we are

Christian Financial Resources to let everyone know right up front what our worldview is and how we're going to run our ministry. The secular world's views of money and wealth are of little interest to us. We want to know what God has said, and he has said plenty. I have a copy of the Financial Stewardship Bible that highlights over 2,000 verses that have to do with money matters. Most people are shocked to know that the Bible talks more about money and how to handle it than almost any other topic. We want to build our ministry on these principles and truths that have stood the test of time.

To appreciate the value of those 2,000-plus verses, think about when you drive on the Interstate. Those big green signs are your best friends, aren't they? Some might argue for the GPS app on their phone, but phones can be lost or forgotten, their batteries can go dead, and sometimes you can't get a signal. But signs never fail you. They tell you which lane to get into, how far down the road your exit is, and what town or city is coming up in case your belly or your gas tank is getting close to empty. Figuratively speaking, we could say that God has placed 2,000-plus signs to direct, assist, and encourage you along the yellow brick road to financial health. Let me tell you about three of those signs that are especially helpful.

Sign #1: God Owns It All

You'll see this sign at the mile marker known as Psalm 24:1: "The earth is the LORD's, and everything in it. The world and all its people belong to him." This is the verse that was front and center in the minds of the people who started CFR over forty years ago. And to this day it is the cornerstone of our financial theology because it makes one thing very clear: God owns everything.

If you watch TV, you know that practically every commercial encourages you to think otherwise. You've seen the once-famous actor telling you that you need to buy gold. You've seen the endless parade of attractive females gesturing at the luxury car that would make you the envy of your friends. And I know you've seen Flo and the gecko and the dude with the emu telling you what a brilliant person you would be if you let them insure all your possessions.

Your possessions.

The world drills it into us over and over again. It's *our* stuff. We *own* it.

But the world is wrong. The earth is the *Lord's* and everything in it.

What does this mean for you and me?

It means we are simply managers. It means that instead of thinking *ownership*, we should be thinking *stewardship*.

Let me explain.

By the time you read this, I will be getting close to being a billionaire. But don't bother looking for me on the Forbes 400 list because I won't be *owning* a billion dollars, I'll only be *managing* a billion dollars. The money our ministry has comes from investors who trust us to manage it well, which makes me a steward. That's pretty easy to understand.

What's harder to grasp is that people who don't have a job like mine are stewards too. People like Jeff Bezos or Elon Musk or the teenagers putting your Chalupa together at Taco Bell. There's a slight difference in their take home pay, but there's no difference in what they own. According to Psalm 24:1, they own nothing. Whatever they have, whether it's a billion dollars or pocket change, they have because God, the owner of all things, has allowed them to manage it for a while. And they will absolutely stand before him someday and give an account of what they did with it.[3]

When you understand that you are a manager and not an owner, and really embrace it, your life will get much better. Why? Because a life focused on acquisition and ownership is always going to be stressful. It's cut-throat, it's about scrambling to meet expectations, and it produces relentless pressure. We even call it the "rat race." Exasperated, we shake our heads and talk about living in a "dog eat dog" world. We say it's a "jungle" out there . . . because it *is* when you're focused on acquisition and ownership. But when you understand that you are simply a manager of what God has entrusted to you, things get much simpler because we have his Word that tells us exactly what to do.

Notice I said that being a manager makes things *simpler*, not *easier*. Simple and easy are two very different things. Simple is when you have a clear path to follow that is unmistakable. We have that. But even on a clear path, there can be challenges and obstacles, as Dorothy and her friends found out on their way to the Emerald City. God never promised us that things would be easy, and I'm certainly not saying that here. In a fallen world where we're always swimming against the current, we're rarely going to experience easy. But God, through his Word, our yellow brick road, has eliminated the need for us to guess or wonder where our next step should land.

Sign #2: God is Generous

I realize you might be feeling a little shell-shocked right now. If you've spent your whole life in acquisition and ownership mode, the news that you don't own anything could come as quite a blow. That's why God put this second sign up in many places all along our yellow brick road. He wants to remind us that, even though he owns it all, he is very generous.

Malachi 3:10 pictures God opening the windows of heaven and pouring out blessings.

Romans 10:12 says that God gives generously to all who call on him.

1 Timothy 6:17 talks about God richly supplying us with good things to enjoy.

You might be thinking, "But wait a minute, Darren. If you looked at my paycheck you would definitely *not* get the impression that God had opened a window in heaven and was pouring blessings on me."

Actually, I think I might.

I've learned that most people are far, far more blessed than they think or feel like they are. To show you that this is not just some happy-sounding platitude that looks good in a book, here's some information you can find with a simple Google search.[4]

If you make just $25,000 per year, you make more money than 90% of all the people on the planet.

If you make the median income for a worker in the United States (about $50,000 per year), you make more money than 98% of all the people on the planet.

Still feeling poor?

Maybe not as much, I hope.

The truth is, you don't own anything but you are still extremely blessed. God may not have buried you in cash, but he's entrusted far more to you than what most people in the world have. And with that yellow brick road to follow, you can manage it in a way that will please God, prompting him to entrust you with even more. Isaiah 1:19 says, "If you will only obey me, you will have plenty to eat." Not *enough* to eat, but *plenty* to eat. We serve a God of plenty, a God who owns it all, but isn't the least bit stingy.

Sign #3: God Can Be Trusted

In the Wizard of Oz, though Dorothy and her friends always had the yellow brick road to follow, there were times when doubts crept in. Like when the forest grew dark and they realized that there were lions and tigers and bears afoot. The temptation to turn back was great, but they decided to trust in that yellow brick road and keep going.

Something similar can happen on our journey to financial health that honors God. We'll see things that seem wrong, that don't make sense, that cause us to doubt. Like poverty, for example. Why does

God give so much to some people and so little to others? Where's the fairness? Where's the justice? Can God really be trusted?

God knew this issue would trouble us on our journey, so he put up some signs. One is a great big billboard in Matthew 25. It's commonly called the parable of the talents, which might seem confusing until you understand that a talent was an amount of money in Bible times. Most scholars believe it was equal to about a year's wage for the average person.

In the story, which was told by Jesus, a wealthy man went on a trip. Before he left he called three of his servants together and entrusted some talents to each of them with instructions to manage the money while he was gone. Interestingly, they weren't equal portions. He gave each of the three guys a different amount of money and offered no explanation as to why. And the servants did not complain. None of them said, "Now hold on just a minute! Why didn't you give me as much as you gave him?" And the reason they didn't question their boss's decision is obvious. The distribution of the money was the businessman's prerogative because it was *his* money! He owned it all so he was the one who got to determine how it was distributed.

This is a powerful reminder for us. God owns everything (See sign #1), so he gets to decide who gets what. It's completely his call.

Right now, you're thinking, "Okay, fine. But that still doesn't explain why he gives so much to some people and so little to others." I would urge you to keep three things in mind.

First, God's ways are very different from our ways.[5] Since the beginning of time, he has done things in surprising, unconventional, often shocking ways. Among other things, he chose the runt of Jesse's sons (David) to be the King of Israel. He chose a young virgin who may have never even changed a diaper to be the mother of his Son, Jesus. And he ordained death by crucifixion to be the capstone of

Jesus's life on earth. None of us would have made those choices if we'd been in charge. So it's hardly surprising that he would handle the distribution of his blessings in a way that seems to make little sense.

Second, God upholds his own established laws, truths, and principles. The law of sowing and reaping is a good example:[6] Two teenagers graduate from high school. One has high ambitions, goes to college, works hard, and becomes a doctor. The other has no ambition, lives in his parents' basement, and picks up an odd job here and there. Though he could if he chose to, God is probably not going to entrust more to the basement dweller than the doctor. He has established certain laws, truths, and principles that govern how this world works and, for the most part, he's going to let them play out.

Third, God knows that money and material things are no measure of love. We have a hard time understanding this because we're so conditioned by our culture to give material things to people to show them how much we love them. Just watch the jewelry store commercials at Christmas time. They flat out say that if you really, really love your wife, you simply *must* buy her that expensive diamond necklace. But God wrote the book on love and knows what a lie that is. He has many ways of loving and caring for people that have nothing to do with money. This is why, if you ever go on a mission trip to a third world country, you will meet people who have almost nothing in terms of material wealth, but are happier, less stressed, and more joyful than you are. It happens all the time. Rich Americans always marvel at the heartfelt joy and laughter and faith that they find in a Haitian church building that has a bare concrete floor, hard wooden benches, and no air-conditioning. Don't ever assume that because a person is poor by the world's standards, he isn't happy and doesn't feel blessed by God.

The bottom line is that, yes, there will be times when we might come to some strange turns in the yellow brick road and wonder if God can be trusted. We might see things that puzzle or trouble us.

The answer is to do what Dorothy and her friends did: just keep going. And keep your eyes peeled for those 2,000-plus signs that God has posted along the way. They will give you wisdom and insight, and reassure you that you're headed in the right direction.

Your First Step

So maybe you're wondering what your first step would be if you decided to follow the yellow brick road. I'm going to give you two assignments that are not optional if you want to be successful in your quest to achieve financial health that honors God.

First, you need to make a list of what God has entrusted to you. Do you have a bank account, investments, maybe a house or some property? Do you have loans, tuition, or other financial obligations? Write it all down. What you'll have when you finish is called a financial snapshot. If you're going to be a manager, you've got to know what you're managing.

Second, write down your spending plan. What is a spending plan? It's a list of your income and expenses. It's how much is coming in versus how much is going out. You would probably be amazed at the number of people who have never given a serious thought to how their spending relates to their income. Even when they're broke, they'll blame the economy or their stingy employer or the high price of goods and services before they'll look at their own habits.

Have you ever tried to walk in total darkness or perhaps with a blindfold on? It's unnerving, isn't it? You take little steps and hold your arms out to feel your way along, and still you crack your shins or stub your toe. What I've just asked you to do with these two steps is the equivalent of turning on the lights or ripping your blindfold off. By creating a financial snapshot and analyzing your income and spending, you're figuring out exactly where you are. You may discover you're in a good place, or you may realize you're nowhere near where you want to be.

I can't emphasize the importance of these two steps enough.

Failing to assemble this information would be like going to a doctor and asking him to treat you without telling him what your symptoms are. He can't possibly know what you need without some critical information. That's how important your financial snapshot and income/expense numbers are. So set aside some time and assemble this information.

As I close this chapter, I want you to think about that yellow brick road in the Wizard of Oz one more time. Do you remember how deserted it was? Dorothy and her friends didn't encounter any other travelers on their way to the Emerald City. Did that ever bother you? I mean, this road led to the Great and Powerful Oz who could make your wildest dreams come true. Why wasn't it jammed with traffic?

I often think the same thing about God's Word. David said that those who read and obey it will be joyful.[7] He said that it gives light in the darkness[8] and makes a person wiser than his enemies.[9] How can it be that so many people, including many Christians, have little if any interest in it?

Jesus said the road is narrow that leads to life, and few are those who find it.[10] He was talking about salvation, but the same thing is true of the road to financial health that honors God. It isn't a crowded road. Never has been and never will be. Most people are on other roads chasing worldly wealth and status. They may not be happy. They may be overworked, stressed out, feeling the pressure to keep up with their peers, and up to their eyeballs in debt, but they're scratching and clawing their way forward, probably because that's all they know.

I want *you* to know that God offers another way.

On a clear road.

To a much better place.

God himself said, "I know the plans I have for you. They are plans for good and not for disaster, to give you a future and a hope."[11]

If that sounds good, there's no better time to take that first step than right now.

QUESTions for Personal Reflection

1) Do you believe God owns everything? If you say yes, what are some things you do that would back up that claim? What are some things you should be doing that you're not? What are some things you should not be doing that you are?

2) We established that most Americans are among the richest people in the world. Why do you think most of us don't feel as blessed as we are? How has the world managed to blind us to God's blessings? Name something you could do that would help you see God's blessings more clearly.

3) What kind of relationship do you have with the Bible, your yellow brick road? How often do you read it? Do you read according to a plan or haphazardly? What are some things you could do to better connect with God through his Word?

4) When you look at your financial snapshot and your spending what changes do you believe you need to make?

CHAPTER 2

Yes, There's a Dragon

It does not do to leave a dragon out of your calculations, if you live near him.

—J. R. R. Tolkien

The Hunt-Lenox Globe is one of the world's oldest globes, dating from the very early 1500s. It is notable not just for its age, but also for three words that the cartographer inscribed on it right along the eastern coast of Asia: *hc svnt dracones*. The phrase means, "here are dragons." There is considerable speculation as to what the words refer to, but they sure do spark the imagination. Literature, mythology, and folklore are peppered with dragon stories, many of which are also quest stories. One of my favorites is *The Hobbit*, by J. R. R. Tolkien.

In Tolkien's fantastically imagined Middle Earth, Hobbits are human-like creatures who stand three or four feet tall, go barefooted, and live in homes that they dig out of the ground. They are generally kind, peace-loving, and very social. Bilbo Baggins, the likable protagonist of *The Hobbit*, becomes embroiled in a quest to help a group of dwarves reclaim their ancestral home, the kingdom of Erebor. They face many dangers along the way, none greater than the terrifying dragon, Smaug, who invaded Erebor 150 years earlier and has held the mountain and its treasure ever since.

Tolkien's classic tale serves as an excellent metaphor for us because the quest to achieve financial health that honors God will bring many people face to face with a particularly unpleasant fire-breathing dragon named "Debt."

According to debt.org, consumer debt in America was almost $14 trillion in 2019. The four key areas where debt just keeps relentlessly climbing are homes, cars, student loans, and credit cards. Speaking of credit cards, the average card holder has four cards and the typical household carries $8,398 of credit card debt.[12] For this reason, countless Americans are financially strapped, struggle to make even the minimum monthly payments on their cards, and worry about their debt issues daily. Ulcers, sleeplessness, irritability, hypertension, and serious relationship troubles are just a few of the problems caused by the debt dragon. No married person who is (or has been) deep in debt will be surprised to learn that money problems are the second leading cause of divorce behind infidelity.[13]

You'd think that with such a horrific history of causing misery, people would run from debt and want nothing to do with it. But no, the debt dragon is actually very seductive. Do you remember how, in *The Hobbit*, Smaug tried to deceive Bilbo with slithery speech and clever lies? Oh, what a cagey creature the debt dragon is! It promises happiness and fulfillment in the here and now and nothing to worry about for a long, long time. But the happiness and fulfillment are never quite as great as you anticipate and the long, long time invariably comes a lot sooner than you expect.

Because you'll never successfully reach the end of your quest to achieve financial health that honors God without defeating this dragon, let me help you understand what you're up against by sharing some pointed questions and answers.

Question #1: Why Is This Dragon So Big?

In other words, why do we have so much debt?

There are a few reasons.

First, our entire culture is set up to encourage debt. The best example of this is the typical car commercial. After showing you how the vehicle will perform spectacularly on a curvy mountain road and go from zero to sixty in less time than it takes to tie your shoe, the voice-over artist informs you that you can take the car home for a shockingly low monthly payment and no interest. Of course, he fails to tell you that you will still be making those payments long after the car has earned "beater" status. According to Edmunds.com, about one third of car owners owe about $5,000 more than their vehicles are worth when they trade them in.[14]

You've probably also received credit cards in the mail with offers of microscopic interest rates, or flyers advertising a blowout sale with a reminder that all major credit cards are accepted. There are also companies like Disney that know you can't afford to fork over the cash for annual passes for your family, so they happily offer to set you up on monthly payments. And on and on it goes. One after another, businesses large and small provide ways for you to have what you can't really afford. Which brings me to the second reason why the debt dragon is so big:

So many people lack contentment. The commercials and flyers and offers mentioned above are effective because large numbers of people feel that something is missing from their lives. And instead of looking inward to figure out what that might be (which is almost certainly where the problem is), they look outward and play right into the hands of the advertisers who are showing them images of deliriously happy people driving beautiful cars, taking exotic vacations, and developing washboard abs on exercise machines that cost more than a month's salary. Who among us hasn't watched those commercials with a hint of longing? Who hasn't heard that little voice whispering, telling us how happy we would be if we could just do that or have that?

Third, the debt dragon is huge because so many people are looking for stress relief. I know about a woman whose husband counted over

100 brand new outfits that still had the tags attached hanging in various closets throughout his house. He said that every time his wife had a bad day, she went shopping.

But it's not just women.

A friend told me about a man who had a garage sale where he sold five sets of golf clubs and over twenty expensive putters. When he was asked how he ended up with so much golf equipment, he said, "Every time I got frustrated with my game, I convinced myself that my clubs were the problem." When asked why he was selling it all, he said, "Because my wife and I are downsizing and trying to get out of debt."

Do you see yourself in any of these reasons? If so, it's time to do some serious soul searching. Your quest to achieve financial health that honors God is doomed if you continue to feed the dragon.

Question #2: Is the Debt Dragon Evil?

You might be thinking, "Okay Darren, I admit I've messed up by going pretty deep into debt. Does that make me a failure as a Christian? Is debt a terrible sin?"

My answer here might surprise you.

Debt is *not* inherently evil.

Several passages make this clear. One example is Deuteronomy 15:6. God was instructing the Israelites on how they should conduct themselves in the Promised Land. He said, "The LORD your God will bless you as he has promised. You will lend money to many nations but will never need to borrow. You will rule many nations, but they will not rule over you." If debt were inherently evil, God would not have instructed his people to lend money to other nations because, by doing so, they would have been leading those nations into sin.

Some people point to Romans 13:8 to try to prove that any kind of debt is a sin. That's where Paul said, "Owe nothing to anyone—except for your obligation to love one another." But a check of the context shows that Paul was talking about relationships, not finances.

I think a much more relevant statement comes from Jesus in Matthew 5:42: "Give to those who ask, and don't turn away from those who want to borrow."

No, the Bible doesn't teach that debt is evil. However, it clearly does teach that debt is dangerous. Proverbs 22:7 says, "Just as the rich rule the poor, so the borrower is servant to the lender." And Proverbs 22:26-27 says, "Don't agree to guarantee another person's debt or put up security for someone else. If you can't pay it, even your bed will be snatched from under you."

Even if the Bible didn't make these statements about the dangers of the debt dragon, we would still know it's dangerous just from our own experience and observations of the people around us. According to court records, 752,160 people filed for non-business-related bankruptcy in 2019.[15] Also, 493,066 properties went into foreclosure.[16] If these numbers seem high, keep in mind that they were unusually low because 2019 was a year when America's pre-pandemic economy was booming. Historically, these numbers are often twice as high or more.

Consider what this means in human terms: the pain, stress, and embarrassment that comes from losing a home or business. Maybe you have experienced this, or someone close to you has. If so, I don't have to tell you how devastating it is. It often takes people years to recover, and I'm talking about emotionally as well as financially.

The bottom line is that debt is like so many things in this world: not evil, but extremely dangerous if not handled properly. Things like guns, sex, medication, cars, and ladders.

Ladders?

Yes, a ladder might be the most dangerous thing in your house. That most helpful of tools leaning up against the wall in your garage kills 300 people a year and puts over 160,000 more in the hospital.[17]

Just because something isn't evil doesn't mean it isn't dangerous.

The key to success with all potentially dangerous things is to understand how to handle them safely. That is certainly true of the debt dragon.

Question #3: Could the Debt Dragon Ever Actually Help Me?

Let me be clear: I believe it's better if you can avoid going into debt. But I will concede that some debts are okay if they pass certain tests. These tests are not original with me.[18] They are commonly shared by those, like me, whose job it is to help people achieve financial good health. But they're always worth mentioning again because there are plenty of people who haven't heard them.

The key is to apply three tests to any debt you are thinking about incurring.

Test #1: Is the item you're borrowing against going to go up in value or help you produce income? One church that CFR has partnered with purchased twenty acres for $15,000 per acre. Just over ten years later, because of explosive growth in the surrounding area, that church sold five of those acres for $100,000 each. Right now, you may be living in a house that's worth much more than you paid for it. Property values can fluctuate, but for the most part, they go up. Not so with automobiles. Unless you're driving James Bond's original Aston Martin's DB Mark III, I'm pretty sure you are *not* driving a car that's worth much more than you paid for it. Automobiles depreciate, and quickly, often leaving people owing more than they're worth and tying their hands financially.

Test #2: Is the item you're borrowing against worth much more than the debt? You'd think it would never happen, but it does. People borrow more money than an item is actually worth in order to buy it. They might be trying to anticipate what it *could* be worth someday. Or maybe someone lied to them or they didn't do their homework. Let me keep this really simple: You should never borrow more than an item is worth.

Test #3: Is the debt load you're taking on manageable on your current budget? The key word here is "current." Far too many people take on loans they simply cannot afford. They tell themselves that they'll be able to make it if they do some serious belt-tightening, if they cut expenses in other areas or make sacrifices. And their intentions may be good. But life is full of surprises. Raise your hand if you've ever said you were going to spend less, only to end up spending more because something unexpected (like a storm, or an illness, or a layoff, or a pandemic) happened. My recommendation is simple: Make sure the debt load you're taking on is manageable without you having to twist yourself into a pretzel to make the payments.

Based on this three-point test there are three items that are *potentially* okay to use debt to acquire:

A house. Typically, a house will go up in value over the long-term, but you still need to be careful. If too much of your income is going to the payment, you can find yourself house rich and cash poor. I generally recommend that no more than twenty-five percent of your income go toward your mortgage payment.

Student loans. A reasonable amount of student loans to secure an education or training that is going to enable you to support yourself and your family for the rest of your life. Notice, I said a "reasonable" amount of student loan. Some college educations are so outrageously expensive that people are still trying to pay them off decades later. That's why it's important to make sure that the amount of the loan and the earning power of the education you're getting make some kind of sense. A rule of thumb I believe in is that your student loan should not exceed what you would expect to earn the first year after graduation.

Business/Investment. Using debt for a real estate investment or the purchase of a business can make sense in certain situations. You just need to be very confident that you have significant cash reserves and your projected revenues are reasonable and not overly optimistic.

Having considered these three tests, we can also now identify some debt-producers that are not okay, that don't pass the tests. Brace yourself. The list would include:

Credit cards.

Furniture.

Time shares.

Boats.

Motorcycles.

Cars.

Yes, cars. You read that right. If you are driving a car you couldn't pay cash for, you are driving a car you can't afford. I know this is counter to the mentality of our culture. Then again, look at the mess the mentality of our culture has gotten so many people into! We're suckered by promises that the good life is available to us at 0% interest with no payments due until after Christmas. Then, seven years later, when we're still making payments on what has become an old car with a leaky transmission and a strange rattle under the dash, we wish we had made a different decision. My point is that by making a wise decision up front—by avoiding debt that is not okay—you can spare yourself a lot of frustration and regret.

Before we move on, let me say this about credit cards, which was tops on my "not okay" list. Common sense dictates that there will be times when you will have to use one. Making a hotel reservation or buying a ticket to a sporting event becomes quite complicated without a credit card. The key is to never pay a dime of interest. This will require you to be careful and thoughtful. You must not be given to emotional actions, such as impulse buying or trying to soothe your unhappy feelings with a shopping spree. I love it when people have their credit card monthly payment auto-drafted each month so that the balance always gets paid off. Credit cards require you to be careful.

Question #4: How Can I Subdue the Debt Dragon?

The obvious first step is to stop feeding it. Stop adding to your debt. Maybe you know someone who has been on a diet for years. He loses and gains, loses and gains, over and over again in a constantly repeating cycle. The problem is not that he hasn't worked out or eaten healthy food. He may have done thousands of push-ups and eaten enough kale to bury a herd of elephants. The problem is that in between those pull-ups and kale salads he's worked in a few gallons of ice cream and some Big Macs. Losing weight and getting healthy requires a lifestyle change, and so does getting rid of debt. You can't be good for a week and then be bad for a week. You have to commit to being good all the time.

By the way, this is the secret to success in just about every area of life. People have problems, not because they're weak all the time, but because they have weak moments. To the degree that you can minimize your weak moments, you can make progress with any problem.

The second step is to take dead aim on the debt you already have. Start paying it down. Don't even consider defaulting on the debt. Many have done this, but it's wrong. The Bible calls people who don't pay their debts "wicked",[19] so don't even go there in your thinking. Instead, make up your mind that you're going do the right thing. There are two ways you can approach paying off debt.

One, you can attack your debts that have the highest interest rates first. Obviously, this will save you the most money. Or two, you can attack your smallest debts first. Dave Ramsey calls this second way the Snowball Method because it helps you gain quick victories and build momentum. In my decades as a financial advisor, I have recommended both of these approaches, depending on the individual and the situation. The key is to be laser-focused. Do it steadily and relentlessly. And when you get a debt paid off, take the money you were using to make that payment and add it to the amount you were using to pay that debt, then apply the combined amount to the next debt on your list. You will be surprised at how fast your debt will start shrinking.

The third step is to take inventory of your possessions, figure out what you don't need, and sell those things so you can pay off even more debt. Earlier, I told you about a man who had acquired five extra sets of golf clubs and over twenty expensive putters. After selling those items, he was able to wipe out one complete debt that he and his wife had acquired. And they were both thrilled; she to get rid of the debt and he to have more room in his garage.

What do you have in your closets or your garage that you really don't need? Here's a hint: If you've gone through an entire calendar year (all four seasons) and haven't used it or even thought about it, you probably don't need it. Also, keep in mind that technology has provided us with countless easy ways to sell things. Almost anyone can do it.

As I wrap up this chapter, I'm thinking about that reader who might say, "This is all really nice, Darren, but you just have no idea how deeply in debt I am. I've been making bad money choices my whole life. I feel like there's no hope for me to ever get out of debt, even if I take all of your suggestions."

Let me show you why there is hope, and lots of it.

In 2 Kings 4, we're told about a widow who came to the prophet Elisha with just the kind of problem I've addressed in this chapter. Her husband had died with lots of unpaid debt, so her creditors were breathing down her neck, threatening to take her two sons and make them slaves. I can only imagine the fear and stress she was feeling.

Elisha, the man of God, gave her some curious instructions. He told her to borrow as many jars as she could from her neighbors and start filling them with the last bit of olive oil she had in a flask. In spite of the doubts they must have had, her sons obediently hustled throughout the area collecting jars, armloads of jars, which they brought home to their mother. When she began pouring oil into them, she noticed something amazing: Her flask wasn't running dry. She poured and poured and poured, filling jar after jar from her single flask. Only when there were no more jars did her supply of oil run out. Elisha then instructed her to sell enough of the olive oil to pay her debts, and then live on what was left over.

I love this story because it reminds me of two things. One, there is no such thing as a hopeless situation as long as God is on his throne. Things may *seem* hopeless. Others might be writing you off. Vultures may be circling overhead. But our God has a long history of rescuing his people. From the Red Sea to a blazing furnace to a lion's den to a desperate widow's empty cupboards, God has shown his power to be greater than any problem we face.

And two, God is most likely to do what *he* can in our lives when we are doing what *we* can. The clear implication of this story is that if the widow hadn't been willing to borrow and fill the jars . . . if she had whined and complained about what was a seemingly pointless task, she wouldn't have gotten her miracle. But when she humbly followed the prophet's instructions . . . when she did her part, God stepped up and did his.

All of this begs the question: If you are diligent in doing the simple things that are within your power, what might God do for you in response? How might he bless you? How might he cause things to work out in your favor?[20] Only time will tell, of course. But considering his long history of muscle-flexing on behalf of his children who are in dire straits, you have every reason to be optimistic.

QUESTions for Personal Reflection

1) If you are in debt, what are some of the "side effects" you have suffered with regard to your health, happiness, or relationships? In what specific ways would your life change if you could get out of debt? What has prevented you from taking on the debt dragon before now?

2) To what degree are you influenced by the avalanche of advertisements that are designed to make you want to spend money? If you are greatly influenced, why do you think that is? What does it say about your current level of happiness if it can be shaken by a sixty-second commercial? What are some specific things you could do to increase your happiness that have nothing to do with money?

3) One of the big keys to paying down debt is to be laser-focused. To what extent is this a problem for you? Do you tend to run hot and cold? Are you typically on again/off again with your spiritual endeavors? If so, what typically derails you? What are some specific things you could do to ensure a steadier, more consistent commitment?

4) Which method of reducing your debt is best in your situation? Paying the higher interest rate loans first or the smallest debts? What is your debt-free day?

CHAPTER 3

What's in Your Wagon?

By failing to prepare, you are preparing to fail.

—Benjamin Franklin

So far, I've mentioned a couple of fictional quest stories (*The Wizard of Oz* and *The Hobbit*) that illustrate important truths. To begin this chapter on saving and investing, I want to talk about the pioneers in early America who traveled west to California. Have you ever really thought about the challenge they faced?

Consider that it's about 2,000 miles from Missouri to the west coast. Can you imagine how long it would take to get there if you were bumping along at two miles an hour in a covered wagon? Think too about the rivers, mountains, and deserts they had to cross, not to mention the outlaws, wild animals, storms, and diseases they had to contend with. Those people were as tough as nails.

In order to succeed in such an arduous quest, those pioneers had to plan carefully. The failure to take enough food or the proper supplies could result in death because once they got beyond Independence, Missouri, there were very few opportunities to restock. Nancy Flagg, writing for the Job Carr Cabin Museum, offers a list of items that would have been found in every covered wagon just starting out, including 120-200 pounds of flour in canvas sacks, 25-75 pounds of bacon, 15 pounds of ground corn, 50 pounds of rice, and 25 pounds of sugar. She says that the recommended weight limit for those covered wagons was 2,000 pounds, with about three fourths of that being food.[21] Today, we're always being asked, "What's in your wallet?" In those days, the critical question was, "What's in your wagon?"

For the person who wants to achieve financial health that honors God, those early pioneers present a valuable lesson. You can't go off half-cocked. You must plan carefully, which means saving and investing for the long haul.

One thing we can say about life is that it's unpredictable. Not a day goes by that people don't have their lives turned upside down by unexpected circumstances. A person is healthy one day and disabled the next; employed one day and laid off the next; riding the wave of success one day and crashing into the rocks the next. When something bad happens—and it will—you need to be financially prepared. So let's think about saving and investing, the two things you can do to prepare for whatever is just over the horizon.

Saving

Rodents are not beloved animals. The squirrel is probably the least despised member of the rodent family because, with its bushy tail, it is at least somewhat cute. There's also the fact that it has at least one admirable instinct: It is a saver. Have you ever heard someone say he was "squirreling some money away" for a rainy day? Squirrels set a great example for people by collecting nuts during the summertime and burying them all over the place so they'll have food during the winter. (They also often forget where they bury them,[22] but we'll leave that discussion for another time.)

Everybody needs to squirrel some money away. I recommend putting six months' worth of living expenses into an emergency fund that is accessible to you at any time. One month's worth should be in a checking account, and the rest should be in a savings account. The most common reason people need to draw on their emergency fund is a severe economic downturn. When the economy is flying high and our employment is secure, we feel pretty good. But the coronavirus pandemic taught us how quickly things can change.

Notice I'm calling this an "emergency" fund. Do you know what an emergency is? You might be surprised at the number of people who don't. I'm referring to the person who sees new tires as an emergency, or worse yet, buying a new TV because football season starts next week. Anything you know you're going to have to buy eventually (like tires) is not an emergency; it's something to put into your budget. And anything that is purely a toy or a luxury item (like a bigger TV) is not an emergency. An emergency is sudden unemployment or your AC going out during the blistering heat of summer. It's a problem that *has* to be taken care of.

Another benefit of saving is the ability to create an opportunity fund. Have you ever been presented with a great opportunity that you couldn't take advantage of because you didn't have the money? Frustrating, isn't it? You see other people jumping in and reaping the benefit while you're stuck on the sideline. An opportunity fund will allow you to jump in too.

In order to save, you can't spend all the money you get. Sounds elementary, but there are lots of people who don't seem to understand this. They get a paycheck and think, "This is how much money I can spend this week." And they do. Then when an emergency happens, they're crying because they don't have the money they need to take care of it. You simply must spend less than you earn. This will enable you to stockpile money.

In Genesis 41, we're told that Joseph, the ruler of Egypt, diligently stockpiled grain to prepare for a famine. The famine eventually came and was so severe the people cried out for help. That's when Joseph opened the vaults. Genesis 41:54 says, "The famine also struck all the surrounding countries, but throughout Egypt there was plenty of food." It's safe to say that people who save are never sorry, but people who don't save will be sorry, sooner or later.

Cash is king when you are on a journey to combat challenges and to seize opportunities.

Investing

A simple way to think about investing is this: You put away money now, believing that you're going to get back more than you put away at some point in the future. The reason you will get back more in the future is because of *interest.* Interest is the money that's paid to you for depositing your money in a financial institution. Interest is good. What's even better is *compound interest.* The simplest way to understand compound interest is to think of it as "interest on interest." In other words, you get interest, not on the original amount of money you deposited, but on the continually growing amount that interest is producing.

For a simple example, consider the following:

It's called "The Rule of 72." If you divide seventy-two by the interest rate you will earn on your investment, the number you come up with is how many years it will take to double your money. For example, let's say you're going to average 9% interest on your investment. If you divide nine into seventy-two, that's eight. So you'll be doubling your money every eight years!

In practical terms, let's say you're on your way to Starbucks to buy a $5 drink and you are 25 years old. That means you can enjoy that latte or you can invest it and have $160 when you turn 65. So what would happen if, instead of having Starbucks five days a week, you only had it two days a week and invested the difference? And what if you did that every week? (By the way, in case you're thinking that 9% is unlikely on your investments, understand that, historically, the stock market has averaged about a 10% return over the decades in a well-diversified portfolio.)

This is why Albert Einstein said, "Compound interest is the eighth wonder of the world. He who understands it, earns it. He who doesn't, pays it."[23] I'm sure you would rather be earning it, so let me offer you some simple investing principles, and then some dangers to watch out for.

Investing Principle #1: Start Now

Young people just getting started in their careers are usually not making top dollar. Add to that the fact that they may be paying for their first apartment or buying their first car. Money is likely tight, which makes it easy to rationalize a delay in investing. "I'm young, I can afford to wait a year or two" is a common refrain. But a year or two often becomes five or ten or more and, if that happens, you will have done yourself a great disservice. Because of the compound interest you didn't get during that time, you will have cost yourself a shocking amount of money. If you talk to people who are approaching retirement age with really tight finances, I will guarantee you the one thing they will all say is that they wish they had started investing sooner.

There's an old Chinese proverb that says the best time to plant a tree was twenty years ago. The second-best time is today. The same is true of investing. Start now.

Investing Principle #2: Diversify

Never put all your eggs in one basket because, if something happens to that basket, you lose everything. Putting your eggs in several baskets lowers your risk dramatically. Notice, I said it *lowers* your risk, not *eliminates* your risk. So many things can happen—pandemics, political upheavals, and even wars—that can affect your investments. But having your money spread out over multiple industries and financial instruments will keep you from being wiped out like so many Enron employees were who had their entire life savings invested in their company when it went under back in 2001.

Investing Principle #3: Adjust as You Go Along

When you're younger, you can afford to take more risk because, if you have a bad year or two, you still have plenty of time to recover. But as you get older, you'll be wise to take less risk. Imagine what a disaster it would be to lose much of what you've gained just as you're approaching retirement.

To prevent this, I recommend something called a Target Retirement Date Fund. It's an investment tool that automatically gets a little more conservative each year as you near retirement. This means you don't have to be constantly remembering to adjust it yourself. You can just live your life and know that it's doing what you need for it to do. Doing this can save you having to pay a fee to a financial advisor for your retirement account.

Earlier in this book I mentioned the parable of the talents in Matthew 25. That's where Jesus tells a parable about three servants who were given money by their master to manage while he was gone on a trip. Two of the servants invested their allotment and returned to their master even more than they were given. The third servant buried his in the ground and returned to his master exactly the amount he was given. If you know the story, you know that the master was furious with the hole-digger but delighted with the investors. Granted, this story is about much more than money management, but a person would have to be blind not to see the connection to our topic: God wants us to do our best with what he gives us. When it comes to money, that means investing.

But there are some dangers to watch out for. Let me mention a few.

Investing Danger #1: Fees.

It will happen. Someone will come along and offer to help you manage your money in ways that are so brilliant you'll have to wear sunglasses. For a fee, of course. I would encourage you to be wary of fees. Remember, when you pay a fee, that means you have less money to invest. Fees can eat up a significant amount of money over time. When you get older and your finances are more complex, you may need to pay someone to advise you, but probably not when you're young. By reading and keeping yourself informed, you can likely open a Target Retirement Date Fund yourself.

Investing Danger #2: Picking the Wrong Financial Advisor

Let's say the time comes when you do need to get some financial advice. There are two ways you can get into trouble.

One is by picking someone who is not competent in the areas you need expertise. You'd be surprised at the number of people who do this. They have a friend or relative who is doing well financially, so they assume the person is savvy when it comes to all things financial, never stopping to think that the person may have just been in the right place at the right time or had a rich uncle who left him a boatload of cash. Believe me, there are lots of rich people who are terrible with money, just like there are lots of skinny people who eat unhealthy and lots of married people who can't stand their spouses. Never judge a book by its cover!

The other way you can get into trouble is by picking someone who is working for himself rather than for you. Your best course of action would be to choose someone who is a fiduciary. The word refers to someone who is a trustee. Notice the word "trust" in there. A fiduciary is bound by law to put *your* interests first. This is what you want. A **Certified Financial Planner**™ professional is required to do this or lose their certification.

I recommend you interview two or three advisors before making a decision. One place to find potential planners with a kingdom mindset is kingdomadvisors.org. Go to the website and put in your zip code to see who is in your area. You want to ask these questions and get the answers in writing:

1) Are you a fiduciary?
2) How are you paid?
3) What are your qualifications?
4) What is your investment philosophy?
5) Have you ever had any complaints filed against you?

Investing Danger #3: Get-Rich-Quick Schemes/ Bubble-Mania

If you're like most people, rarely a day goes by that some kind of get-rich-quick scheme (or scam) doesn't cross your path. As you're driving in your car you might hear about gorgeous lakefront property in the mountains for an unbelievably low price that you could turn around and sell for twice as much. Or in your email you might receive information about a can't-miss investment opportunity that is sure to make you rich. But of course, you have to act *now*. Schemers and scammers will always encourage you to act hastily. The last thing they want is for you to think and do research.

And then of course there are various manias that sweep the country and get people into big financial trouble. In the 1600s, something called "tulip mania" happened in Holland. Tulips, especially those that bore specific color combinations in the petals, were considered luxury items and status symbols. As the demand for these flowers increased, growers charged higher and higher prices. To give you an idea of how ridiculous things got, imagine people in America today paying $500 for a single tulip bulb. Insane, you say? Nothing like that would ever happen today? Oh, but it does! As recently as the late 1990s in America, tech stocks were overvalued the way tulips were in the 1600s in Holland. I know people who lost as much as seventy-five percent of their investments from those peak stock prices when the tech bubble burst. Beware of any investment that has you feeling pressured or desperate to hurry up and take the plunge because you're afraid of missing out on something incredible. This is the very definition of bubble mania! I recommend you take time to pray about any investment before you actually make it.

Never forget that investing is about the long haul. It's the consistent plodder who achieves prosperity. People who are always grabbing at this or that red hot opportunity are bound to get burned, and probably sooner rather than later. Proverbs 21:5 says, "Steady plodding brings prosperity; hasty speculation bring poverty."[24]

Investing Danger #4: Letting Fear Drive Your Decisions

Using scare tactics is the oldest game in town. Have you ever taken your perfectly running car in for an oil change and had the mechanic tell you that you need hundreds of dollars-worth of work done? He starts listing all the terrible things that could happen to you out on the road if you don't let him change out a half dozen parts.

Something similar happens in the investment industry. There are ads being run as I write these words suggesting that if you don't have millions of dollars socked away, you'll never be able to retire. This is terribly misleading because it's a blanket statement that fails to take into consideration important factors such as your age and lifestyle and the amount of money you might be able to make in retirement. But when people are scared, they make emotional, often hasty, ill-advised decisions. Schemers and scammers love it when people react out of fear.

Investing Danger #5: Taking on Too Much or Too Little Risk

I've already mentioned this, but it bears repeating. Some people (usually those who are younger) are costing themselves money by playing it too safe, while others (usually those who are older) are risking disaster by not playing it safe enough. Remember, the younger you are, the more you can afford to take risks because you have time to recover if you have a bad year or two. The older you are, the more you need to protect your gains because you *don't* have time to recover if something bad happens.

As I close this chapter, I want to share a personal conviction I have about retirement. There is a mindset that sees retirement as the time of life when a person is finally able to withdraw from all obligations and just live a life of self-indulgence. For example, a newly retired school teacher might be approached by her pastor to teach a new class that's starting up at church. Her response is, "Nope. I taught for thirty-two years. I'm done with that!" Talk to any pastor and you'll hear stories about church members who play golf five or six days a week, but refuse to help out at church.

My plea is for you to understand the value you have in your golden years. You bring knowledge and wisdom and experience to the table, all of which are sorely needed in every church. You likely have people skills and leadership skills that have been honed over decades. I can think of few greater tragedies than for people with so much to offer the Kingdom to just check out and live solely for themselves. It's as if we have battalions of soldiers that have turned in their weapons and are playing cards in the barracks instead of helping to fight the war.

Don't be one of them!

Even if your saving and investing accumulates a mountain of money, there is still a war going on and you are needed.

QUESTions for Personal Reflection

1) How would you rate yourself as a saver? As the old saying goes, does money "burn a hole in your pocket" or do you "squirrel it away" for a rainy day? If you're not a good saver, can you identify the reason for your weakness? (Do you try to "keep up with the Joneses?" Are you a sucker for any cool new product?) What is it that needs to change in your heart to help you improve in this area?

2) Have you started saving and investing yet, or have you been telling yourself that you're still young and have plenty of time? If you haven't started yet, think about your income and ask yourself how much you could set aside each week. Is there something you could do without and never miss? Is there a small lifestyle change you could make that would produce a huge benefit years down the road if you were to invest that money today?

3) How do you view your retirement years? Do you see them as a "promised land" of total freedom and self-indulgence, a time when you can quit all your obligations and only do what you want? Or do you see them as an opportunity to cut back on worldly obligations so you can do more for the Lord? How do you think God views your retirement years?

4) What is the best investment you have ever made? What is the worst investment you have ever made?

CHAPTER 4

We Don't Call Them "Wise Men" for Nothing

We make a living by what we get.
We make a life by what we give.

—Sir Winston Churchill

Astrologers live with their eyes on the sky. They know the stars like a pianist knows the keys of his instrument or a doctor knows the body of his patient. And so it was that, a little more than two-thousand years ago, some astrologers in Persia noticed a star among the constellations that was unusually bright. It wasn't distinctive enough to stir the masses into a panic by sparking fears of an alien invasion, but it was bright enough to catch those stargazers' attention and make them wonder if they were looking at the fulfillment of a prophecy found deep in the Old Testament: "A star will rise from Jacob; a scepter will emerge from Israel."[25]

Through the promptings of the Holy Spirit, God revealed to these men, known to us as the Magi or "Wise Men," that the star would lead them to the newborn King of Israel. And so they set off on a quest to find and worship him. Without question it is one of the most famous quests in history, one that we commemorate every Christmas season in music, art, and drama. The reason I mention the Wise Men here is because they really were wise; wise enough to seek

Jesus and to grasp a critical truth that escapes many Christians, that worship and giving go hand in hand. When they knelt before Jesus at the end of their quest, they were bearing gold, frankincense, and myrrh, costly gifts that came in handy for a poor young couple that was about to flee to Egypt in order to escape the bloodlust of the maniacal King Herod.

Primarily because of the Wise Men, gift-giving is a part of our Christmas celebration. When I was a kid, like every other kid, Christmas excited me. I couldn't wait to see what I was going to get. But now, as a grown man with a wife and children of my own, I find Christmas even more exciting because I've discovered a great truth that I didn't know when I was young: Giving is a deeper, richer experience than receiving. When I see the looks on my wife and children's faces as they open their gifts, the thrill I feel is far greater than anything I ever felt as a kid when I opened a gift. That thrill is exactly what Jesus was talking about when he said that it is more blessed to give than to receive.[26] He wasn't belittling receiving, he was exalting giving.

Time and time again I'm reminded of the blessedness of giving. A number of years ago, Journey Christian Church in Apopka, Florida, asked its members to give generously so that a new and much-needed building could be built. I and lots of other people happily gave to that project because of our love for the church and our belief in its mission. I'll never forget the Sunday morning our pastor asked everyone to stand who had been drawn to the church, started attending, or accepted Christ at least partly because of the new building. I got chills as I saw people rise to their feet all around the auditorium. Many of them I had met. Many of their baptisms I had watched. I will guarantee you that every person in attendance that day who had given generously to that project felt an inexpressible joy.

Giving is one of the most thrilling, satisfying, and meaningful things you can do. Unfortunately, a lot of people—including a lot of Christians—still haven't made this discovery. Why?

One reason is because they've been hoodwinked by a materialistic culture into believing that happiness and success are found in the acquisition of things rather than the giving of them. Do you realize that current estimates have the average American being exposed to between 6,000 and 10,000 ads per day?[27] You can't watch a baseball game anymore without seeing ads on the backstop. You can't open your weather app without seeing an ad right alongside the forecast. And what do you think those thousands of ads are saying? They're *not* saying that you'll move closer to the happiness you've always dreamed of if you become a generous giver. They're saying that you'll move closer to the happiness you've always dreamed of if you buy what they're selling. And for good measure, they employ your favorite celebrities and sports stars to show you what kind of cool fraternity you'll be joining if you buy their product. Thousands of times every day it is pounded into our brains that happiness comes from acquiring, not giving.

A second reason why so many Christians haven't discovered the joy of giving is because of fear. We know life is uncertain. We knew it even before 2020 gave us a pandemic that killed millions and wrecked our economy. And it's this knowledge, this fear of uncertainty that causes a lot of people to cling tightly to their money. They don't see it as being stingy, they see it as being wise. They say, "You just never know what might happen. I want to be prepared." And they're right, but only to a point. If your financial plan doesn't include giving, you become like the man Jesus called a fool, the selfish man who built bigger barns to hold all of his stuff and never gave a thought to how he might be able to help people with his wealth.[28]

In this chapter, I want to go against the grain of what our culture believes and promotes. I want to challenge you to take a hard look at your giving habits and offer some ideas on how you might step up your game, because one thing is certain: Your quest to achieve financial health that honors God will never be completed until you become a giver.

Three Kinds of Givers

Some people are completely selfish and tightfisted and rarely give anything to anybody. We can put them in a category all by themselves. The rest of us, those who *do* give, fall into three different categories: givers, generous givers, and radical givers.

A *giver* is someone who gives safely. He knows there are many needs and he's happy to make a contribution, but not without checking his bank balance first. He carefully calculates and measures to make sure he doesn't stretch himself too thin. He may even be a tither, but if he is, he will see the tithe (one-tenth of his income) as an obligation to fulfill rather than a place to start.

The *generous giver* is less calculating. He has a tender heart and is often moved to outbursts of generosity that go above and beyond what the typical giver would consider wise or safe. It might be a missionary's testimony or a natural disaster that touches his heart. He might hear that a coworker has been laid off or that a struggling young family on his street has incurred a lot of medical bills and feel compelled to help. But don't make the mistake of thinking that all generous givers are wealthy; they're not. Some of the most generous people I've ever met have been people of very modest means. It's not the size of their bank accounts, but the size of their hearts and their faith that makes them generous.

And then there's the *radical giver*. This is the person who gives so generously that many people would swear he's crazy. In the Bible, Zacchaeus is such a person. You'll recall that he was a crooked tax collector who became wealthy by overcharging people and keeping the excess for himself. But one day, he had lunch with Jesus and everything changed. We don't know what Jesus said to him, but it must have touched him deeply because he came out of that meeting a changed man, promising to give half of what he owned to the poor and to pay back everyone he had ripped off four times as much as he extorted.[29]

Let that soak in.

We would be impressed if he just made a commitment to quit overcharging people. Even more impressed if he decided to make a nice contribution to the poor. But paying back everyone he had stolen from four times over? Giving half of what he owned? That's crazy, isn't it?

No, it's radical.

Every generation produces a few radical givers who are generous to a degree that seems shocking. The key word in that sentence is "few." Why are radical givers so rare? More to the point, why aren't more Christians radical givers? I would say it's because so few believers have had a true "Zacchaeus moment." So few have had an encounter with Christ that is so profound that it has reshaped the landscape of their life.

Let's face it: A lot of people go to church every Sunday, sing songs and listen to messages without ever having a profound encounter with Jesus. They hear a lot about him. They may *know* a lot about him. But they have never offered him the throne of their hearts. They've never surrendered enough of themselves to him to allow for a truly life-altering change. This is what I pray for, the desire that fuels my life's work. I can only imagine how the Kingdom of God would explode, how it would transform the world if more non-givers became givers, and if more givers moved up to the next level and became generous givers, and if more generous givers moved up to the next level and became radical givers.

Where do you fit in?

Being totally honest, if you had to fit yourself into one of these categories—nongiver, giver, generous giver, or radical giver—which would it be? I challenge you to spend some time reflecting on this question. In my experience, a lot of people think they are more generous than they really are. Some people think they deserve a medal if they give a dollar out their car window to a homeless person on a street corner. I'm not saying that everybody has to be a radical giver, though I think everybody could be. However, I do believe every Christian ought to at least be a generous giver. The apostle Paul instructed Timothy to teach, not just giving, but generosity to his people: "Tell them to use their money to do good. They should be rich in good works and generous to those in need."[30]

No More Excuses

I'm a fan of Kansas City sports teams, so I have really been enjoying the Chiefs since Patrick Mahomes came along. There are many people who say that the Chiefs' success is almost entirely because of Patrick Mahomes. But I know—and you can be sure Patrick Mahomes knows—that no quarterback can win games by himself. He needs a good offensive line and skill players and a great defense and special teams to be a champion. Success in sports is a team thing, not an individual thing.

The same is true in the Kingdom of God. A few super Christians with deep pockets will never be able to accomplish as much as multitudes of ordinary Christians who decide to be generous. The problem is that ordinary Christians who live paycheck to paycheck sometimes find it easy to make excuses.

"I can barely pay my bills as it is."

"I haven't had a raise in two years."

"My kid is getting braces next month."

"My car is on its last leg."

And every pastor's personal favorite: "I'm a little over-extended right now, but just you wait and see. When I get out from under some of these bills I'm going to be generous with the church."

It's so easy to hear statements like this and nod sympathetically. I mean, who doesn't have sympathy for people who are struggling financially? Often, it's not even their fault. The problem is that there's always someone who comes along and torpedoes the assumptions that keep these classic excuses afloat.

In the first church capital campaign I was a part of all the way back in the middle '90's, I met a single mother with three kids. She wanted to give to the campaign but her budget was so tight she couldn't find even a spare nickel beyond her regular weekly offering. So she decided just to pray for the campaign instead of giving.

One day her children came home from Sunday School all excited. They had heard a lesson about sacrificial giving and asked their mom what sacrifice they could make as a family so that other kids could hear about Jesus. After a lengthy discussion, they decided as a family that the only way to come up with some extra money would be to cancel their cable TV subscription and give that money to the campaign instead. They all agreed, and ended up giving the campaign $1,530 over the next three years. It was one of the smallest gifts but it impacted the entire church.

I tell that story often when I speak to churches because I know that in every congregation there are people who have convinced themselves that they just can't be generous. They look at that bank account balance and say, "Nope, no way." But there's always a way. Jesus made it clear that there's always a way when he told the story about a poor widow who put everything she had into the Temple treasury.[31] If ever a woman could have made an excuse, she could have. Instead, she chose, not just to give and not just to be generous, but to be radical in her giving.

Be honest. Have you been an excuse-maker when it comes to

giving? Have you let the fact that money is tight keep you from even trying to be generous? If so, it's time to face the truth. There *is* no excuse for not giving generously.

Simple Ideas for Maximizing Your Giving

At CFR, we're all about encouraging people to give, especially people who have decided they want to give, but don't have a history of giving and, therefore, don't have good habits established. So let me wrap up this chapter by giving you some practical suggestions that could very well move you up to the next level in your giving.

Suggestion #1: Strive for Consistency

In every area of life, consistency is a key to success. Couples that are divorcing will tell you that they get along okay sometimes, they just don't get along consistently. People who fight with their weight will tell you that they eat healthy food sometimes, they just don't eat it consistently. And on and on it goes. It's the haphazard, hit-and-miss, up-and-down approach to any lifestyle choice that keeps us mired in mediocrity.

When it comes to giving, you'll do much better if you're consistent. The key to consistent giving is making a one once-and-for-all decision to give and then sticking with it rather than having to decide all over again every week. If you have to make the decision to give all over again every seven days you will become a slave to whatever crisis happens to be brewing at the moment or whatever storm cloud is looming on the horizon. "I better hold off on my giving this week because that insurance payment is coming up." Trust me, there will always be a reason not to give.

One way you can establish consistency in your giving is to do it online. Many churches now offer online giving, which can be set up to automatically make your contribution every week without you doing a thing. Even if you're sick or traveling and can't make it to church, your contribution will be made. Not only does this simplify your life, it blesses the church by providing income that is steady and dependable.

Of course, the question of how much to give always comes up. The Bible teaches percentage giving and mentions the tithe (one tenth) specifically, but my dream is to motivate more people to give not ten percent, but twenty percent or more of all the blessings God gives them. Because we're all going to be blessed according to our level of generosity,[32] it only makes sense to give more, not less. God in his infinite wisdom seems to encourage percentage giving to remind us to give back as he blesses us more. What percentage are you giving away each year of your total income?

Suggestion #2: Utilize Tools that Have Been Created to Help You

An excellent example would be a tool that CFR and some other financial institutions offer. It's called a Donor Advised Fund, or more commonly, a "giving fund." A good way to think of it would be as a charity checking account. Very simply, you put money into the account and then draw on that money when you want to make a "grant" to a church, mission, or other qualified charity. The money you put into the account can be cash, stock, or other assets. While it is in the account, it draws tax-free interest and, if you use CFR, the dollars are helping churches. At any time, you can designate a qualified ministry or charity you would like to give a grant to and a gift will be made on your behalf.

What are the benefits of giving this way?

First, you get the maximum tax deduction allowed by the IRS if your giving fund is held by a 5013C charity. Second, you have the option of giving anonymously or of having your name printed on the check. Third, record keeping for your taxes is much easier because you get one receipt from your fund holder. This means you don't have to run around tracking down receipts from every mission or charity you give to. Fourth, you can view your giving fund online and make deposits or grant recommendations at any time. And finally, your giving fund creates a legacy of generosity for you and your family.

Naturally, you will have questions beyond what I'm able to answer here, and you can get answers to those questions by visiting our web-site[33] or giving us a call. My purpose here is simply to show you that there are amazing tools that have been created to energize and maximize your giving. When you take advantage of them, you take your giving to a whole new level. Always remember, giving is the one investment that will pay off 1,000 years from now.

Suggestion #3: Be Strategic

One way to give strategically is to think in terms of assets other than money. You may not have a lot of cashflow, but you could have possessions that have value. Second homes, antique cars, horses, empty lots, baseball card collections, jewelry, and even time and talent have been converted into money that has helped the Kingdom. And nothing is more biblical! Acts 4 says that in the early days of the church people routinely sold personal possessions and brought the money they made to the apostles.[34]

Or maybe you own some stock. Did you know that when you give appreciated assets like stock to a charity you never have to pay any taxes on the gains, which means you can give more?

You might also be surprised to know that business owners can give part ownership of their business into a giving fund to save taxes and leave a legacy. Even royalties on a book can be given. For example, 100% of the royalties on this book are going into a giving fund!

Finally, our ministry has consulted on hundreds of generosity initiatives in churches. Often, we are able to find a generous giver that will anonymously offer to match whatever the rest of the church gives in their kick-off weekend. Leveraging a gift like this is shrewd for both the giver doing the match and the giver that is seeing their gift doubled.

The key here is to be creative, to think strategically. Don't just give robotically. Put your thinking cap on. Ask God to show you ways to maximize your giving.

I want to close this chapter with a true story that appeared in the Panama City New Herald in July of 2017. Roberta Ursrey and her husband, mother, nephews, and sons were enjoying the beach one afternoon when, suddenly, she noticed that her boys were farther from the shore than seemed safe. As she walked toward the beach to call and motion for them to come in, she heard their screams. They were caught in a riptide.

Roberta's instinct was to dive in and go after them, but everyone was warning her that to do so would endanger her life as well. Still, she couldn't just stand there and watch her family drown, so she ran and dove into the water. Predictably, she too quickly came under duress and it appeared that the entire family might drown.

That's when Jessica Simmons who, with her husband, had decided to enjoy a beach-side lunch, realized what was happening and sprang into action. She started organizing total strangers into a "human chain" that stretched from the beach all the way out to where the Ursrey family members were fighting for their lives. In all, over eighty people joined hands to make the chain. And yes, the entire Ursrey family was saved.

That story is powerful on many levels, but I love it because it shows the life-saving power of many people combining their efforts. That's exactly what happens in the church when Christians pool their resources through faithful, generous giving.

Please don't skim over this truth too quickly.

There are people who are lost today that could hear about Jesus and accept him, and that you could actually meet in heaven someday because you were a faithful, generous giver.

Imagine their gratitude.

Imagine your joy.

Imagine the smile on God's face.

It's my belief that giving is often the last point of struggle people face when it comes to surrendering to the Lord. You've heard the old joke about the guy who held his wallet up out of the water so it wouldn't get wet when he was baptized. Are you one of those people who loves Jesus and worships and serves, but has never become a generous giver? Have you been a willing recipient of God's blessings for years without ever truly challenging yourself to reciprocate? If everybody in your church practiced the same level of generosity that you do, would the church have to scale back its ministry? Would it have to close its doors?

The answers to these questions will tell you what you need to do.

QUESTions for Personal Reflection

1) Have your thoughts about giving and receiving changed since you were a child? If so, how? What (or who) do you think is responsible for that change?

2) If you have not been a generous giver up to this point, can you pinpoint why? Are you materialistic? Do you fear the uncertainty of the future? What role should your faith play in helping you work through these obstacles to generous giving?

3) In what category would you put yourself: nongiver, giver, generous giver, or radical giver? Can you think of a time when you felt moved to go above and beyond your normal giving without being asked?

4) Have you been an excuse-maker when it comes to giving? When the subject of giving comes up, are you quick to mention all the reasons why it's hard for you right now? Have you made promises to do better without actually ever doing better?

5) How would you rate yourself when it comes to giving consistently? Does your giving tend to fluctuate according to your emotions or your bank balance? Can you think of some tools you aren't taking advantage of that would help you be a better giver?

CHAPTER 5

A Yoda You Should Be

What you do is your history.
What you set in motion is your legacy.

—Leonard Sweet

You never forget the first movie you see in a theater. For me it was Star Wars. I was a wide-eyed five-year-old when my sister took me to see it. I went home that day with images in my head that were brand new and incredibly exciting. I dreamed of being on an intergalactic quest like Luke Skywalker. Even now, after all these years, I have deep affection for the Star Wars movies.

It was in the second movie, *The Empire Strikes Back*, that arguably the most beloved character in the entire series makes his appearance: Yoda. Yoda is small, green, male, and of an unspecified species. He is old—900 years old to be exact—which means he has been around long enough to have experienced much of the galactic history that supports the films. He is also the most renowned Jedi Master, known for his uncommon wisdom and mastery of the skill of lightsaber combat.

The reason I'm mentioning Yoda at the beginning of this last chapter is because he is the perfect example of what it takes to complete your quest for financial health that honors God. Having lived out his own 900-year quest, Yoda was committed to passing on his knowledge and experience to help the younger generations of Jedi.

This is where so many of his uniquely phrased sayings come from, such as:

"Do or do not, there is no try."

"When you look at the dark side, careful you must be.
For the dark side looks back."

"If no mistake you have made, losing you are.
A different game you should play."

When it comes to our finances, we all have a responsibility to do what Yoda did, to think about the next generation (our kids) and what we can do to give them the best opportunity to succeed in *their* quest to achieve financial health that honors God.

One way to think about this is to picture a track and field relay race. There is a baton that has to be passed. The passing of that baton, whether it's done smoothly or clumsily, often determines the outcome of the race. If you want some chuckles, do an Internet search on the words "worst baton pass ever." The videos you'll see will be cringe-worthy. You'll see world-class sprinters who have trained for years experiencing catastrophic outcomes because of botched handoffs. As Christians, the last thing we want to do is make good financial decisions that honor God and then fail in the "handoff" to our children.

Or perhaps you have built a sandcastle at the beach. I'm not talking about moving some sand around with your hands and calling it a castle. I'm talking about going all out, spending hours painstakingly shaping the sand and creating the wall, the keep, and the battlements. If you have done this, then you know the sense of accomplishment that comes when you finish. Imagine yourself stepping back to admire your handiwork just as your son or daughter, chasing an errant beachball, comes crashing into it, destroying the whole thing. Sadly, this is a picture of what happens in many families when it comes to finances; what is built by one generation is destroyed by the next.

When I teach seminars, I love to ask people to raise their hands if they feel their parents did a good job of teaching them how to handle money. Sadly, the number of hands raised is always a small minority.

In Scripture, there is much talk about the importance of people imparting their wisdom and experience to the next generation, and the next generation accepting and embracing that wisdom. Solomon said, "My child, listen to me and do as I say, and you will have a long, good life. I will teach you wisdom's ways and lead you in straight paths. When you walk, you won't be held back; when you run, you won't stumble. Take hold of my instructions; don't let them go. Guard them, for they are the key to life."[35]

Allow me to suggest three goals you should have as a parent that will enable you to help your children in their own financial quest.

Goal #1: Make Sure You Are Adequately Insured, but not Over-Insured

Buying insurance is like buying tires: it's not fun. You're not getting anything pretty or exciting or worth talking about around the water cooler at work. But when you find yourself on a rain-slickened road, you're sure glad you've got those new tires, and when life hits you with an unexpected expense, you're sure glad you've got insurance. The trick is to find that perfect balance of being adequately insured, but not over-insured.

One thing you must remember is that insurance is for catastrophic events. Remember this when you are standing at the counter of your local electronics store buying an item that costs $150 and the checkout person asks you if you would like to purchase an extended warranty. Your answer should be no. Chances are, the item will work just fine for a long time. But even if it doesn't, an item costing $150 going on the blink is not catastrophic. What *is* catastrophic?

Another car rear-ending you at a stoplight.

A grease fire that destroys your kitchen.

A storm that drops a tree onto your house.

An illness that puts you in a hospital.

An injury that disables you.

For such things as these, you probably need insurance. I say "probably" because there are some people who are financially secure enough to handle some of the losses mentioned above, or to "self-insure." And as your net worth grows, you may be able to self-insure more. But if you do need insurance for these things, be careful not to over-insure. There are numerous ways this can happen.

One is by adding riders to your policy. A rider is an additional benefit that is added to your insurance policy that you pay extra for. Insurance companies offer just about every kind of rider you can think of, such as paying your beneficiary more money if you die accidentally instead of by a natural cause. Riders often sound good when first presented, but keep this in mind: They cost you money and make the insurance company money. Insurance companies love riders. So read the fine print and make sure you really need one. In many cases, you won't.

Another way people become over-insured is by paying a higher premium to have a lower deductible. Let's say you're paying extra every month to have a low $500 deductible, as opposed to a $1,000 deductible on accident repairs for your car. If you can afford a $1,000 deductible in the case of an accident, you'd be very wise to stop paying extra for that $500 deductible. Month after month after month of paying extra for a low deductible that you may never use (and don't really need) might make your insurance company love you, but it won't help your finances at all.

Obviously, the key to being adequately insured without being over-insured is to get good counsel. Find a broker you know and trust, or one that is recommended by someone you know and trust. Do your own research to make sure what you're being told is accurate. Avoid ideas that sound gimmicky or too good to be true. And above all, keep up with your insurance policies. As you move into different stages of life, your insurance needs will change.

Goal #2: Create a Legacy Plan.

Also known as an "estate plan," a legacy plan, in simple terms, is a plan for how to resolve certain key issues at the end of your life. What will happen to your assets when you're gone? (Taxes may hit you and your beneficiaries hard if you don't have a plan.) And before you're gone, do you want to be kept on life support? And if so, for how long and under what circumstances?

Unfortunately, lots of people die without a legacy plan. When it happens, it's probably *not* because the person never heard of wills or trusts or estate planning. Most likely, it's because of procrastination, or because the person simply didn't feel comfortable thinking and talking about his own mortality. I'll agree that death is not the happiest of topics, but as Christians we should know that this world is not our home.[36] We should look forward to the day when we get to meet our Savior face to face and receive the rewards he has promised us. If thinking and talking about your departure from this world is a problem for you, I encourage you to read and meditate on the promises of God concerning heaven. If you need to, talk to someone—perhaps your pastor—and work through whatever is troubling you.

The good news is that when you get ready to make a legacy plan, you'll find lots of help available. The ministry I lead, Christian Financial Resources, will help you at no cost if you are leaving money to Christian entities through your giving fund. We'll also advise and encourage you to invest in the Kingdom by leaving a percentage of your estate to one or more worthy Christian organizations of your choice. I see this as being of critical importance. If you truly want to leave a wonderful legacy, you can't do better than investing in the Kingdom of God so that future generations can know Christ. With the psalmist, Asaph, you can say, "We will tell the next generation about the glorious deeds of the LORD, about his power and his mighty wonders."[37]

While I'm on this subject, I want to address a problem that often arises in the area of estate planning that is nothing short of tragic. It's well illustrated by a story a pastor friend told me about a funeral he officiated for a man who had several grown sons. When his sons and their families arrived at the church for the service, there was a strange tension in the air. Ordinarily, bereaved family members are hugging and wiping tears and even clinging to each other. In this case, the brothers were glaring at each other like boxers getting their final instructions from the referee. Suddenly, the pastor heard shouting in the foyer. He rushed to the scene and found the funeral home personnel physically separating the brothers before fisticuffs broke out. The pastor learned later that the animosity sprung from the reading of the will. There was bitterness and resentment over the choices their father had made, and much suspicion that one of the brothers had secretly manipulated his father into making decisions that heavily favored him over his brothers.

Countless family feuds have been triggered by legacy plans, perhaps leaving you to wonder how you can ensure that *your* legacy plan doesn't turn into a powder keg that could blow up and tear your family apart after you die. This is especially worrisome to people who have children who are Christians and others who are not. This fear might even cause some people not to make a legacy plan at all.

Obviously, all families are different, and it's true that some types of people will never be happy no matter what the will says. But I have an idea that I believe will foster peace among your heirs after you die. I recommend writing a love letter to your spouse and/or children and attaching it to the documents. I also recommend sitting down with your family and talking about the choices you've made and why. If you have created a giving fund (see previous chapter) you could explain to your loved ones why you did it and what churches, ministries, or missionaries you would like to see receive money after you're gone. Most of the time, when you see families torn apart by a will, it's because no one knew what was coming. Assumptions were made and perhaps carried for years, only to be exploded without warning.

To stretch this idea even further, I recommend sitting down with your family to discuss these things every year, perhaps at Christmas time, to reaffirm your love and to inform them of any updates or changes to your legacy plan. Not only will doing this strengthen the bond of love between you and your closest family members, it will also relieve them of the worry and uncertainty so many people experience when their spouse or parents are aging and they have no idea what arrangements have been made. Most of all, it will eliminate any surprises for your loved ones after you're gone. If they have concerns or questions, you'll be able to talk them through. They'll be able to hear straight from you why you made the choices you did instead of wondering what you were thinking after you're gone.

Romans 14:19 encourages us to pursue those things that make for peace. When you make a legacy plan and lovingly share it with your family, that's exactly what you'll be doing.

Goal #3: Teach Your Children What You Have Learned on Your Quest.

Speaking of quests, parenting is quite an adventure in its own right. I don't think anybody really has a clue how weird and wonderful the experience will be until that first child actually arrives. Prospective parents read books, search the Internet, listen to podcasts, and digest a river of information that flows into their ears from family and friends. But when the baby arrives, a lot of it goes out the window and they find themselves hanging on for dear life.

If you're a parent, pause for a moment and ask yourself a question: When you find yourself nearing the end of your life and you think about your children, where will your mind go? What will seem important to you?

Will you recall that Little League trophy your son won when he was twelve?

Will you glory in that first dance recital your daughter had when she was seven?

Will their high school diplomas fill you with pride?

Will you rest easy when you think about all the big promotions they got over the years?

I doubt it.

I'm guessing your thoughts will be focused on the kind of people they are, the quality of the lives they're living, and most of all, whether or not they know the Lord. Individual achievements will mean little if you see your children on a road that dishonors God.

There are so many moments in our lives as parents when we feel overwhelmed. Life comes at us fast, there are so many decisions to make and crises to handle that we feel like we're caught up in a tornado. Then, suddenly, the nest is empty, the kids are gone, and we're wondering what happened. Don't let the opportunity to teach your kids valuable truths slip through your fingers. Don't let the day-to-day hustle and bustle of family life distract you from teaching your children what they need to know to live lives that honor God.

And yes, finances are a part of that. All the way back in the introduction to this book I told you that only 29% of Americans feel that they are financially healthy. Of the 71% that feel they are *not* financially healthy, you can be certain that a good many are not honoring God with their money. Further, you can be sure that other spiritual problems are growing out of the mess their finances are in: worry, overwork, a lack of generosity, envy, poor self-esteem . . . the list goes on and on. Please don't think that just taking your kids to church or sending them to church camp is enough. You must be intentional about teaching them what you have learned about life.

When I was pursuing my MBA, I did a massive research project on family-owned businesses. I learned several surprising facts, but perhaps the biggest was that most family-owned businesses don't survive the third generation. That means that if your grandfather started a successful business and passed it on to your father who then passed it on to you, there's a better than fifty-fifty chance that the business is going to die while in your hands. When that happens to any business, doesn't it make you wonder what *wasn't* passed on from one generation to the next? Buildings and products and customers were, of course. But what about core values and principles and standards?

One of the most important passages of Scripture in the Bible is known as "the Shema." *Shema* is a Hebrew word that means "listen," which is the first word of the passage which starts in Deuteronomy 6:4. You've probably heard it. It says:

> Listen, O Israel! The LORD is our God, the LORD alone. And you must love the LORD your God with all your heart, all your soul, and all your strength. And you must commit yourselves wholeheartedly to these commands that I am giving you today. Repeat them again and again to your children. Talk about them when you are at home and when you are on the road, when you are going to bed and when you are getting up. Tie them to your hands and wear them on your forehead as reminders. Write them on the doorposts of your house and on your gates.[38]

Did you notice that middle section where it says to repeat the commands of God again and again to your children? And to talk about them throughout the day, wherever you go and whatever you do? No, I don't think that means that if you take your son to a baseball game, you should be lecturing him about the importance of not being over-insured during the seventh inning stretch. But it does mean that as you make your way through life with your children, you should be seizing whatever teaching moments might come unexpectedly and intentionally creating a few of your own.

One thing I have done with my kids is to give them an allowance each month, starting at the age of eleven. We put a certain dollar amount times their age onto a Bluebird card (an American Express debit card with virtually no fees) each month. By doing this we teach them to share, save, and spend. They share by giving ten percent to our church, they save by putting ten percent into a savings or investment account, and they are free to spend the remainder on their clothes, snacks, entertainment, etc.

Another simple idea would be to create a family giving fund where, as a family, you research Christian ministries that are doing great work, discuss them, and decide together which ones you'd like to support. What a fantastic way to expose your children to great Christian servants and get them excited about giving.

Finally, I buy each of my kids their first stock when they turn thirteen. Some parents might even want to match dollar for dollar every investment a kid puts in their Roth IRA for their first job. It's so important to teach them the power of compound interest at a young age!

The key is to make leading and teaching your children a commitment, a mindset. It's all about making a decision to do whatever you can to ensure that your children know everything you have learned about living a life that honors God.

As I wrap up this last chapter, I want to make an important point about parenting that will encourage you. Yes, passing on Godly truths to our children is a big responsibility. And yes, there are many forces working against us. It's easy to feel intimidated. But keep this in mind: When your children are young, they *want* to be like you.

My own son is a perfect example. We adopted him from Russia when he was eighteen months old, which means he and I don't share a biological heritage or roots in Kansas. Other than those first eighteen months, he's lived his entire life in Orlando, Florida. But would you like to guess who his favorite baseball and football teams are? That's right, the Kansas City Royals and the Kansas City Chiefs. Do you wonder how such a coincidence happened? Of course you don't! You know without me telling you that he picked up on my love of those teams and wanted to be like me. That's right, he *wanted* to be like his dad.

He's become like me in other ways too. He loves to watch financial news on TV, which is very unusual for a boy his age. And he doesn't dance. When this was noticed by some girls at his last homecoming dance, they asked him about it. His response was, "I don't dance when the stocks are down." (It had been a rough week on Wall Street.) I laughed when I heard that one. The kid is a regular Mini-Me.

The point is, our children are wired to *want* to be like us when they are young. Which means you have a wonderful opportunity, a wide-open window to teach them to make godly lifestyle choices. The mistake many parents make is waiting too long to start. They think a four-year-old is too young to learn about things like saving and giving and planning. If this thought has crossed your mind, I suggest that you turn on your TV to one of the networks that caters to children and watch the commercials. You'll find that the advertisers are investing millions to teach your children about spending and acquiring in a steady stream of 30- and 60-second commercials. They *know* your kids can learn; it's time you believed it too, and started leading them in the right direction. I plead with you to reflect on the Shema. Think about how you can weave God's truth into your daily interactions with your children. They're ready to learn if you're ready to teach!

QUESTions for Personal Reflection

1) What is your general feeling about insurance? Are you risking financial disaster by refusing to buy it, or are you so heavily insured that your insurance broker has a picture of you on his refrigerator? How often do you review your insurance needs? Do you know exactly what coverages you have?

2) Do you have a legacy plan? If not, why? Do you have a hard time talking about end-of-life issues? If so, can you be specific about why that is? Is there someone you could talk to that might help you overcome your hesitation?

3) If you have younger children, name some things you're currently doing that are designed to help them learn how to manage money wisely. Are there other things you could do? How diligent are you when it comes to seizing spontaneous teaching moments that come up throughout the day? Can you commit to being more attentive to these opportunities?

4) Did your parents teach you well about handling money? What is your biggest struggle when it comes to managing money? What, specifically, can you do to keep from passing that weakness on to your children?

A MESSAGE FROM DARREN

I have always been a guy who trusts God. Oh, I have weak moments like everyone else, but for the most part I do trust him. But when "COVID" hit, I was spooked, big time. Visions of disaster started dancing in my head because we make loans to churches so they can build buildings and expand their ministries. Suddenly, churches across the country were not able to meet together, which I thought would result in their incomes being slashed, which meant they wouldn't be able to make their loan payments. I also pictured thousands of our investors being furloughed or let go from their jobs and needing to withdraw their money. And, because churches were closed, I knew our team wouldn't be able to travel and speak, which is a key component in our growth strategy. I am not exaggerating when I say that the last two weeks of March, 2020 were the most stressful two weeks of my life.

But I worried for nothing.

It gives me chills to tell you that the second quarter of 2020 was the best quarter in the forty-year history of our organization. Our previous record for investments in one quarter was $28 million. In the second quarter of 2020, with COVID rampaging and almost every business and church in the country shutting down, we accepted investments worth $43 million. Something like this is only possible because God is bigger than whatever problems we face, and because he is faithful to his people.

In Deuteronomy 31, the Israelites were ending their forty-year sojourn in the wilderness and were preparing to invade the Promised Land. Moses was at the end of his life and Joshua was ready to take over. Moses made what amounted to a farewell speech, and he did so knowing that the people were still extremely nervous about the nations living in the land they were about to enter. Those tribes were to them what COVID was to me, the thing that struck fear in their hearts. So Moses chose his words very carefully. In Deuteronomy 31:6, he said, "Be strong and courageous! Do not be afraid and do not panic before them. For the LORD your God will personally go ahead of you. He will neither fail you nor abandon you."

He will neither fail you nor abandon you.

This is the message I want to leave you with. If your finances are a mess . . . if you feel hopeless every time you look at your bank account, God is your answer. He's given you a path to follow and all he asks is that you get on it and stay on it. Follow it in good times and in bad. Follow it when it's easy and when it's hard. Follow it when slick talkers are trying to lure you onto a different path. I can't tell you how long it will take for you to find the "Holy Grail" of financial health that honors God (everybody's situation is different), but I can promise that it *will* happen because he will neither fail you nor abandon you.

Or maybe your finances are in okay shape, but you know in your heart that you haven't really honored God with your money. Maybe he's blessed you with a really good job, but you've never committed to becoming a generous (or, dare I say, radical) giver. Whichever situation you're in, there's a better way to live. A more meaningful way. A happier way. A more blessed way.

I pray that you'll begin your quest today, that you'll be faithful and never give up, and that someday you'll stand before God and hear the seven most beautiful words that will ever fall on human ears: "Well done, my good and faithful servant."[39]

I'd love to hear from you. You can reach me at:

darren@cfrministry.org

—Darren Key

ACKNOWLEDGMENTS

This book would not have been written without my friend and partner in ministry, Mark Atteberry. His prodding, sifting through my notes, and countless Zoom calls helped me get this book out of my head and onto paper. Thank you, Mark. You deserve an extra jewel in heaven.

Thanks also to Acorn Publishing for making things easy for this first-time author. Holly and Jessica were fantastic to work with and moved the process along in a timely fashion, producing an outstanding finished product.

Finally, I am grateful to the CFR ministry team. I am surrounded by a group of dedicated coworkers that impact hundreds of thousands of people in our mission of "funding ministry . . . changing lives." My CFR team members are too numerous to mention, but Mike Kocolowski, Tim Stephens, Jose Maldonado, and Tiffany Pawson deserve special mention for serving faithfully alongside me for over 10 years.

Finally, I am thankful to God for his love, grace, and mercy. And for his message of truth that I am privileged to carry to the world.

ABOUT THE AUTHORS

Darren R. Key

Darren Key is the CEO of Christian Financial Resources (CFR), one of the largest and fastest growing church extension funds in the country with a mission of "funding ministry . . . changing lives". Darren has a Bachelor Degree in Christian Service from Manhattan Christian College, a Bachelor Degree in Business Administration (Finance) from Kansas State University, an MBA from the University of Louisville, and is a CERTIFIED FINANCIAL PLANNER™ professional. Darren is married to Rachel. They have four kids: an adopted son named Alex from Russia, adopted daughter named Scarlett from Kyrgyzstan, and twin biological girls named Amelia and Juliette.

Mark Atteberry

Mark Atteberry is the author of fourteen books, including *The Samson Syndrome* and the multiple award-winning suspense novel, *Dream*. You can learn more about his work at:

alittlestrongereveryday.com

ENDNOTES

---

1 https://www.forbes.com/sites/donnafuscaldo/2019/11/15/most-americans-struggling-financially-despite the strong-economy/#4ee0b9444b6b

2 1 Timothy 6:17-18 (NASV)

3 Romans 14:12

4 howrichami.givingwhatwecan.org

5 Isaiah 55:8-9

6 Galatians 6:7

7 Psalm 119:2

8 Psalm 119:130

9 Psalm 119:98

10 Matthew 7:14

11 Jeremiah 29:11

12 https://www.debt.org/faqs/americans-in-debt/

13 https://www.daveramsey.com/pr/money-ruining-marriages-in-america

14 https://www.edmunds.com/car-buying/being-upside-down.html

15 https://www.statista.com/statistics/817911/number-of-non-business-bankruptcies-in-the-united-states/

16 https://www.housingwire.com/articles/foreclosure-filings-fell-to-a-record-low-in-2019/

17 https://www.nachi.org/ladder-safety.htm

18 The Crown Financial Small Group Bible Study is where I was introduced to these ideas.

19 Psalm 37:21

20 Romans 8:28

21 https://www.jobcarrmuseum.org/blog/oregon-trail-foods-preparing-for-the-journey

22 http://sciencenetlinks.com/science-news/science-updates/squirrel-hoarding/

23 https://quotesonfinance.com/quote/79/albert-einstein-compound-interest

24 Quoted from the Living Bible

25 Numbers 24:17

26 Acts 20:35

27 https://ppcprotect.com/how-many-ads-do-we-see-a-day/

28 Luke 12:16-21

29 Luke 19:1-10

30 1 Timothy 6:18

31 Luke 21:1-4

32 Luke 6:38

33 cfrministry.org

34 Acts 4:34-35

35 Proverbs 4:10-13

36 Philippians 3:20

37 Psalm 78:4

38 Deuteronomy 6:4-9

39 Matthew 25:23

Made in USA - Kendallville, IN
74496_9781952112683
08.20.2022 1315